What's a Sequencer?

By
Greg R.
Starr

**A basic guide to their
features and use.**

 Hal Leonard Publishing Corporation

Library of Congress Cataloging-in-Publication Data

Starr, Greg R.
What's a sequencer? : a basic guide to their features and use / Greg R. Starr.
   p. cm.
   Includes index.
   ISBN 0-7935-0083-4 (pbk.)
   1. Sequencer (Musical instrument) -- Instruction and study.   ·
  I. Title.
MT192.S8 1990   90-53369
786.7'6--dc20   CIP
                                                    MN

ISBN 0-7935-0083-4

Library of Congress Card No. 90-53369

First printing September, 1990

Contents

Introduction:
Do I need a degree in computer science to operate a sequencer, and if so, what's wrong with playing my old penny whistle anyway?

ASKED YOURSELF THIS QUESTION LATELY? Does it seem as if the march of technology is giving you blisters? Not even sure if you want to get your boots on? Well, tie up those laces. Using the latest music technology isn't magic and doesn't require a Ph.D. in electrical engineering or rocket science. A little patience, a smidgen of knowledge, and a little hands-on experience are all you need to get the most out of your sequencer, whether you have a single-track recorder built into your portable keyboard or a full-blown 200-track program loaded into your personal computer.

A sequencer will open new horizons in your musical creativity, making it possible for you to play with a band that you create, to capture and alter your performances, and to write out your music with greater ease than ever before.

MANY NAMES, WORK THE SAME

Sequencers come in variety of forms and are known by many names. But whether they are called "Performance Recorders," "Music Programmers," "MIDI Sequence Recorders," or simply "Sequencers," they all perform roughly the same function. Their sole purpose is the storage of incoming data (information) for playback through a compatible instrument. Wow, does that sound like a lot! For now, think of a sequencer as a fancy electronic tape recorder that will record the notes you play into it.

Most sequencers today are *MIDI* sequencers (Chapter 4 explains what this means). Consequently, much of this book is devoted to using such units with electronic keyboards and other MIDI-compatible equipment. But it's worth noting that some sequencers built into portable or home keyboards don't "speak MIDI." Chapter 3 addresses these built-in sequencers specifically, although much of the rest of the book is applicable to them as well; *all* sequencers—MIDI or not—operate according to the same principles.

If you own a sequencer, this book will cover both the basics of using it and the more advanced "goodies" that are available on some models. If you don't have a sequencer and are thinking of buying one (or a keyboard with one built in), you'll find enough information here to ask the right questions and decide which model is right for your particular needs.

So please come in, take your shoes off. We'll get you some moleskin for those blisters. You can check your penny whistle at the door.

1

So, what is a sequencer?

PEOPLE HAVE ALWAYS BEEN FASCINATED by machines that play music. Music boxes and player pianos have always had an attraction for most people. Just take a peek into a music box shop at a local shopping mall. People stand and marvel at these wonderful little devices that plunk out their favorite songs. They will stand for long periods of time and smile when they finally remember the name of the tune they are listening to. (Children often play for hours with a simpler version of the same thing: the jack-in-the-box.)

These incredible contraptions are really mechanical sequencers. Notes are played back after "programming" them by sticking pins into a drum or disk. The notes are played back at a rate determined by the speed of the disk or drum. Speed up the music box, the music gets faster. Slow it down and the music gets slower. Notice, though, that in both speeding up and slowing down the mechanism, the pitch of the notes doesn't change. Slowing a music box down isn't the same as slowing a record down, where the speed of the record determines the pitch. This distinction will be important to the discussion of sequencers in the following chapters.

A familiar mechanical sequencer.

Just like a music box, a player piano is a type of mechanical sequencer. A pianist plays the piano while a roll of paper runs through a mechanism that punches a series of holes in it. During playback, the piano "reads" these holes and plays the appropriate notes. And just like the music box, speeding up the piano roll doesn't change the pitch of any note that is played. It only changes the speed at which the notes are played back.

WHAT IT IS, WHAT IT DOES

So, what is a sequencer, anyway? How does a sequencer fit into a home system for making music? What can a sequencer do for you? Well, in current jargon, a sequencer is a device that will record and play back performance data (information). Okay, fine. But what will it do for you, and why do you need your data recorded? Well, what if you had the sounds of an entire band at your fingertips and could record each part separately, then play them all back simultaneously while you played along? Or if you were writing a piece of music and decided that instead of piano, you'd like to hear it with strings? Or what if you are all fumble-fingered but have some great musical ideas that you want to hear? All of these things are possible with a sequencer. Through the use of a sequencer, you can experience the joy that making music is supposed to be.

2

If I see a sequencer on the street, how will I recognize it and what should I say to introduce myself?

TODAY'S SEQUENCERS ARE ELECTRONIC, rather than mechanical, in nature. And they come in a variety of forms. Some are dedicated hardware units—boxes whose sole purpose in life is to record and play back musical information. Others are built into electronic keyboards—augmenting the list of sounds and other capabilities that such instruments possess. Still others don't exist as physical objects at all, but instead are programs that are run on personal computers.

No matter what form they come in, sequencers all perform the same function. They all record what is played into them and then play it back for you. This in itself isn't particularly earth-shattering. An ordinary tape recorder can do the same thing. So what makes a sequencer so special?

A MAGIC RECORDER

Imagine a tape deck on which it is possible to record not one, not two, but many separate parts—up to 16 or more. It would be possible to record a piano part, then go back and record a separate string part. While listening to these parts, go back and play a bass guitar part, and so on. You can create your own band, all by yourself.

This is one thing that makes a sequencer special. From your keyboard, it is possible to record many individual parts and have them play back simultaneously. Create your own orchestra from the ground up, always at your beck and call, waiting to play the music you've created.

A sequencer is most easily thought of as a "magic" tape recorder. Most of the controls are the same ones found on a tape deck. Play, Record, Stop, Pause—these are controls you probably are familiar with. They do the same job, whether on a sequencer or a cassette player. If you want to play a sequence, press Play. If you want to record into the sequencer, press Record. The basic operation of the machine is the same, whether tape deck or sequencer.

There are some distinct differences, however. Don't try to sing into a sequencer. It won't do any good. It will only record performances from a keyboard or, in the case of a MIDI sequencer, possibly from some other MIDI controller, such as a MIDI drum pad or guitar synthesizer. A sequencer doesn't record sound. It only records incoming data. These data aren't sound at all. They are strictly information about a performance, not the sound of the performance itself.

Think about the piano roll mentioned in Chapter 1. The roll of paper won't make a sound, short of a crinkle or a rip. It stores the data needed by the player piano to reproduce the music. A sequencer stores the data that a keyboard, or other sound source, needs in order to reproduce the music. The sequencer won't make any sound by itself; only when it is connected to a sound source. All of this data tells the connected instruments what to play.

Sequencers also let you play back the recorded data at a tempo different from the original speed. Ever play a 33 r.p.m. record at 45 r.p.m.? Sounds pretty silly! A sequencer, on the other hand, will let you play back the data at any tempo within the sequencer's range, without changing the pitch of the song. The note data aren't changed, just played faster or slower. This can be pretty handy for those of us who aren't virtuosic on the keyboard. A difficult piece or section of music can be recorded at a slow tempo, then played back at a faster one. Impress your friends and relatives with your keyboard prowess! Only you need to know the secret.

Imagine taking a piano roll off of a player piano and putting it on a player organ instead. Or a player harpsichord. Because the performance information recorded on the roll isn't the actual sound of the performance, that information can be played back on a different instrument than was used for recording.

The situation is similar with electronic sequencers. You can play back the same notes on a different instrument, or a different sound on the same instrument. If you don't like the piano part in a piece, try it with strings instead. Try that with a tape recorder!

The following chapters will look at a number of possible configurations of sequencers and how they can be utilized at home, starting with the most basic: a single keyboard with a built-in sequencer.

3

Sequencers on portable and home keyboards, or How did they sneak that thing in there without my seeing it?

FOR MANY MUSIC HOBBYISTS (as well as a number of professional players), home and portable keyboards are the ideal do-it-all instruments. With their variety of instrumental sounds, drum rhythms, and easy-to-play automatic accompaniment, they are the contemporary answer to the one-man bands of yesteryear. When you add a sequencer to this equation, the result can be a pretty enticing instrument.

More and more keyboards are designed with sequencers built right into them. They aren't all operated in exactly the same way (so it's important to read the owner's manual carefully), but they all record and play back in some fashion. They come under a variety of names, but they all are similar underneath the hood. They just come in different colors and have different optional features.

There are two main categories of sequencers built into home keyboards:

- Those that record only on a single part, often called a track. Depending on the model of keyboard you have, you can record automatic accompaniment (easy-play chords and automatic rhythm) or melody notes into this track. Or you may be able to record both automatic accompaniment and a melody line into this single track at the same time.

- Those that have multiple tracks for you to record on. Again, depending on the model of your keyboard, the types of information recorded into a track will vary. It may be only automatic accompaniment, only melody notes, or both at the same time.

ONE-TRACK MIND

Operation of a one-track sequencer is straightforward:

1. Press the Record button.

2. Record the designated part into the sequencer. If the sequencer records easy-play chords and automatic rhythm, play the chords, with the rhythm running, while the sequencer records. If the sequencer records a melody line, play the melody line while the sequencer records. Or record both melody and accompaniment if your sequencer has this capability.

3. Press Stop.

4. Press Play to play back the recorded part. In the case of sequenced chords and rhythm, you can play a melody "live" while the sequenced part plays back. Or if you have prerecorded the melody and accompaniment, play a countermelody or duet part along with the sequenced parts.

MULTIPLE TRACKS

Sequencers that record more than one part are often called *multitrack* sequencers. These allow you to record two, three, or more parts onto individual tracks. A typical four-track sequencer has controls labeled SOLO (for single-note melody), ORCHESTRA (for a second melodic or chordal part), ACCOMPANIMENT (for easy-play chords and automatic rhythm), and BASS (for a bass line). Only data from the designated keyboard regions can go into these tracks.

	Record	Play
SOLO	[●]	[○]
ORCHESTRA	[○]	[●]
ACCOMPANIMENT	[○]	[●]
BASS	[●]	[○]

A typical four-track built-in sequencer.

You can set each track to record or play back independently of the others. Two columns of lights tell you which tracks are set to record and which to play back.

A more sophisticated sequencer is becoming more common on newer home keyboards. It is also a multitrack sequencer, but instead of designating tracks for specific things, such as solo or bass, any type (or types) of information can go into these tracks. Select the track to record on (up to ten tracks on some models) and record the part. You can set each track to record or play back separately, just like the other type of multitrack sequencer.

Along with the note data, many sequencers are "friendly" enough to record tempo changes, the voice or sound selection, and other control settings automatically. Such automatic recording of front panel settings is a great idea, making the sequencer easy to use.

TINY SEQUENCERS

A type of "micro-sequencer" is also available on some home keyboards. These small creatures will record one and only one type of information. They come under variety of names, but they are sequencers none the less:

- *Registration memory* will record front panel (registration) information.

- *Custom drum programmers* allow you to construct your own drum patterns, typically one or two measures long, which can then be played back over and over, the same as any of the preset rhythm patterns.

- *Custom accompaniment programmers* go a step beyond drum patterns to allow you to record your own automatic chord and bass patterns.

These younger cousins can be very handy critters, being able to recall at the touch of a button an entire front panel setting or a drum or accompaniment pattern you have created.

LITTLE BOXES

A recent trend for manufacturers is the production of home model, external sequencer units. These little black boxes (well, okay, so they're not all black) are very friendly and easy to use. Generally, they are designed for specific instruments from one particular manufacturer. The whole idea behind home sequencers is recording your music with a minimum of muss and fuss. The less difficulty you have in using them, the better the manufacturer has succeeded. These sequencers use MIDI to communicate with an instrument. The following chapters discuss MIDI sequencing in greater depth.

4

The road to MIDI

WHAT IS MIDI, AND WHY SHOULD YOU CARE? Before
answering this question, let's take a few steps back and peer
into the dark regions of history before MIDI came into being.

ANA-ONE, ANA-TWO

Sherman, set the Wayback machine for the early days of
synthesizers (early 1970s). These early *analog* synths were
controlled by variations in voltage. (Suffice it to say that the
higher the voltage that went into the sound generator, the
higher the pitch that was generated.) An analog sequencer, as
part of this control-voltage system, would spit out
preprogrammed voltages to the sound generator to produce a
series of notes. These sequencers could typically produce only
16 different notes, and each note had to be tuned individually
by turning a knob or moving a slider. These modules, though
advanced for the time, quickly developed a reputation for
sounding dull and mechanical. Incessantly repeating patterns
played over and over became less novel and started sounding
boring and dated. Just over the horizon, however, were the
first *digital* sequencers.

DIG IT ALL

The first digital sequencers were a blend of the then-new digital (computer) technology and the old analog (voltage) technology. They combined digital memory with control-voltage outputs to create a digital/analog hybrid. These new units solved two of the biggest limitations of the old analog modules, namely the number of notes and tuning. They had digital memory, which expanded the note capacity to 250–1000 notes, depending on the model. They could also be calibrated so the output voltages that drove the sound generators were very accurate. (The old analog units were notoriously inaccurate and hence notoriously out of tune.)

On the earliest of these sequencers, as on their analog predecessors, you had to specify the pitch of each note one at a time—a procedure known as *step-time* input. Later models allowed you to actually sit down at the keyboard and play (imagine!) while the sequencer recorded—something called *real-time* input. But even this new blend of technologies had its shortcomings.

Imagine yourself recording into a sequencer. You have been trying to record a piano part for the past two hours. You are just playing the last flawless phrase when Fido, the faithful family dog, decides that he wants to show his undying affection by giving you doggy kisses. Of course, this interruption causes you excessive anguish because in the process of receiving these enthusiastic doggy kisses, you make a blatant mistake in the part you were recording. With most of the digital/analog hybrid sequencers, editing (changing) a single event such as a wrong note was impossible. The only option after Fido's emotional outburst was to rerecord the entire part from the beginning. Editing a single event, such as a wrong note, simply wasn't possible.

Not only was editing a problem, but compatibility was also an issue. Brand X's sequencer might or might not work with Brand Y's synthesizer (most likely not). Only certain sequencers would work with certain keyboards, usually from the same manufacturer. These systems, although powerful for the time, were doomed to extinction when the MIDI specification was developed.

AND THEN ALONG CAME MIDI

In 1982, a common language was adopted by manufacturers of keyboards and synthesizers that is called MIDI (the acronym for "Musical Instrument Digital Interface"). MIDI is a language that keyboards and other compatible equipment speak to each other, allowing them to communicate.

So what's the big deal? Imagine you are at the United Nations. A monumental decision has been made that all communication at the UN will now be made in a common language. No matter where you are from, you can communicate with anyone that is at the UN in this common language. Well, that is what MIDI did for synthesizers and keyboards. No matter what manufacturer made the keyboard, it can communicate with any other MIDI-compatible keyboard or device (like a sequencer!!!). No longer is a user limited to any one manufacturer or system. You now can mix and match equipment to suit your particular needs.

MIDI is arguably the most important advance in music since the invention of music notation. It is impossible (very difficult, at least) to escape, and it has made music making both more powerful and more enjoyable for the general public.

If an instrument doesn't speak MIDI, you won't be able to play it from a MIDI sequencer. A non-MIDI instrument won't understand what the sequencer is trying to tell it. It also won't have a MIDI port (a fancy word for a connection) on the back.

YOU SAY DAYTA, I SAY DATTA

So far, we've talked a lot about sequencers recording data. But what types of data are they? What kind of information gets recorded into a sequencer track? Well, first of all, notes are recorded, along with a "time stamp" that tells the sequencer when to play a particular note. But what else? Music is more than just a string of notes played at the right time. There must be more in a track than just that. Well, there is. Here are other kinds of data that your sequencer will record:

- **Note Length.** The sequencer will record how long each key is held down. A note will continue to sound for that length of time. When a key is pressed, the keyboard sends a message to the sequencer saying, "This key is down now." When you release the key, the keyboard will send a message to the sequencer saying, "This key is up now." Upon playback, the sequencer will tell the keyboard or sound module to play and "hold down" that note until it tells the keyboard to release the note.

- **Key Velocity.** This is the speed at which a key gets pressed. Usually, the faster a key is played, the louder the note sounds.

- **Pitch Bend.** If your keyboard has a pitch bend wheel or lever, your sequencer may be able to record its movement. Pitch bends on such instruments as flute or sax can be very effective. Your sequencer may allow you to edit that pitch bend as well, if you didn't get it quite right the first time.

- **Controller Data.** This category is a bit of a catch-all. Controller data can be a number of different things. When you press the sustain pedal, for example, the keyboard sends out a controller message. This message is recorded by the sequencer. Upon playback, the sequencer transmits this controller message back to the instrument along with the note data, triggering the sustain function.

20

The modulation wheel ("mod wheel" for short) is another common controller. Modulation is often used to add vibrato to notes. If your keyboard has such a controller, your sequencer may record its motion and allow you to edit it, too. There other controllers as well, but these two are the most common.

- **Patch Change.** Within a single track, it is possible to program the sequencer to change sounds for you. Instead of reaching over to the instrument and changing sounds (commonly called Patches) by hand, you can have the sequencer do it for you. Using patch changes, it is possible to change the sound of a track in mid-stream.

Okay, enough of this "data" stuff. Let's get our hands dirty and hook up some equipment and see what we come up with.

5

"Can we hook things up now?" and other important questions

YOU HAVE BEEN VERY PATIENT SO FAR. If you are the typical MIDI user, the first thing you want to do with a new piece of equipment is use it. Rare is the person who reads the manual and only then plugs the new toy in. Well, you've waited long enough. Let's rip open some boxes and hook the gizmos up.

There are a number of different configurations that you can employ when setting up a MIDI system that includes a sequencer. Your setup will depend upon the equipment you have. There are, however, some general guidelines to follow:

- MIDI OUT ports are connected to MIDI IN ports. MIDI OUT transmits MIDI information; MIDI IN receives it. (By the way, connections are made with MIDI cables, which have identical connectors on both ends.)

- MIDI THRU ports are connected to MIDI IN ports. MIDI THRU passes along the information coming into the MIDI IN port. You'll see the usefulness of this in the discussion of various system configurations.

23

SIMPLE SYSTEMS

The simplest system is a keyboard with a built-in sequencer and no external modules. It is self-contained and requires no external MIDI connections at all. Plug in the keyboard and go. These systems can not only be small portable or home keyboards, as discussed in Chapter 3, but also full-blown professional "workstations."

Next, you could hook up an external module to your single keyboard. This module could be a drum machine, a tone module, or another keyboard. The keyboard from which you record is called the *master*; the external module is called the *slave*. To set up this system:

- Connect the MIDI OUT of the master to the MIDI IN of the slave.

- Next, connect the MIDI OUT of the slave to the MIDI IN of the master.

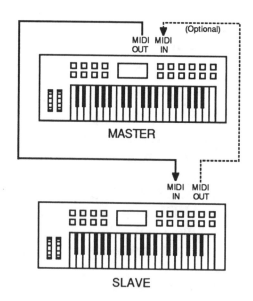

Master keyboard with one slave.

This second of these connections is optional. If you decide to make only the single connection, note that the slave cannot talk back to the master keyboard. There is no data line going from the slave to the master. This usually isn't a problem, unless you wish to record into the sequencer from the slave. You may wish to do this if the slave is, for example, a drum machine.

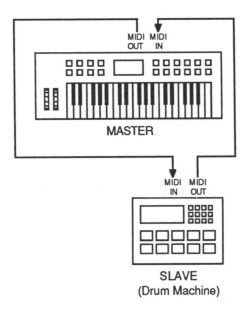

Two-way connection for recording from the slave.

MORE SLAVES!

You can complicate things a little bit more by adding another slave to your system. But where do you connect it? Don't panic! This is where the power of the MIDI THRU port comes into play. Remember that the information coming into a module gets passed on to its MIDI THRU port. The information passes THRU the instrument unchanged (hence the name). To add another slave to your system:

- Connect the MIDI OUT of the master keyboard to the MIDI IN of the first slave.

- Connect the MIDI THRU of the first slave to the MIDI IN of the second slave. The information going to the first unit will go into it, as well as pass through the MIDI THRU port to the second unit.

- If more modules are involved, continue to daisy-chain them together using the MIDI THRU ports.

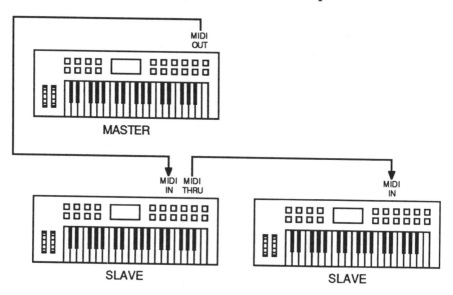

Daisy-chaining multiple slaves.

INTERNALIZING THE EXTERNALS

What happens when you have an external sequencer and not a built-in model in your keyboard? The connections will be similar to those of the master keyboard/slave module setup.

To hook up a system with a hardware sequencer and a single keyboard:

- Connect the MIDI OUT of the sequencer to the MIDI IN of the keyboard.

- Connect the MIDI OUT of the keyboard to the MIDI IN of the sequencer.

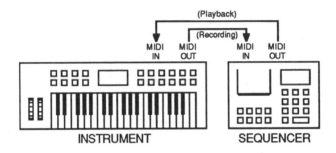

Connections for one instrument and an external sequencer.

This system differs slightly from the master keyboard/slave module setup. Both connections are necessary in this case. MIDI data must be able to go from the sequencer to the keyboard. Without this connection, the keyboard will receive no data from the sequencer and will make no sound when you try to play the sequence. Likewise, data must be able to go from the keyboard into the sequencer. Without this connection, no data will get into the sequencer and therefore nothing will be recorded by it.

OVER, UNDER, OUT, AND THRU

If you will be using several modules, it may be worthwhile to look into a MIDI THRU box, or at a sequencer with several MIDI OUT ports. A THRU box provides multiple MIDI OUT ports from a single MIDI IN port. Daisy-chaining can result in some instruments down the chain responding erratically. A THRU box, or multiple MIDI OUT ports, will solve this problem.

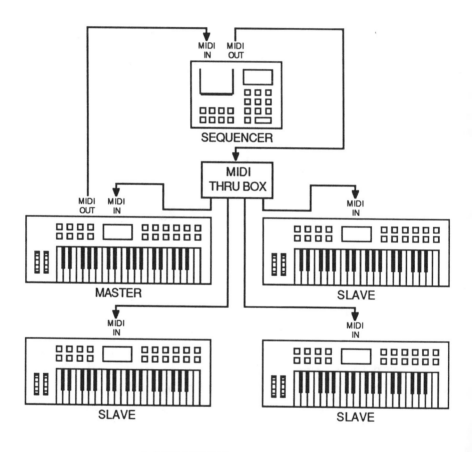

A MIDI THRU box in action.

use a MIDI THRU box:

- Connect the MIDI OUT of the sequencer to the MIDI IN of the THRU Box.

- Connect the MIDI OUT of the master keyboard to the MIDI IN of the sequencer.

- Connect a MIDI OUT from the THRU box to the MIDI IN of the master keyboard.

- Connect all the slave instruments to the THRU box by connecting the MIDI OUTs from the box to the MIDI INs of the slaves.

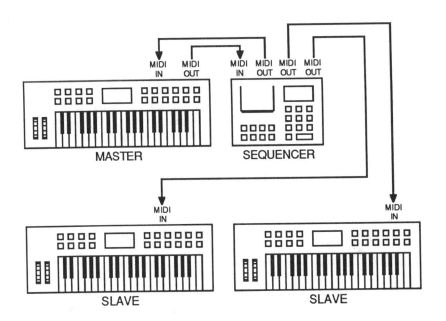

Using a sequencer with multiple MIDI OUTs.

To hook up a sequencer with multiple MIDI OUT ports:

- Connect the MIDI IN of the sequencer to the MIDI OUT of the master keyboard.

- Connect a MIDI OUT from the sequencer to the MIDI IN of the master keyboard.

- Connect all the slave instruments to the sequencer by plugging the MIDI OUTs from the sequencer into the MIDI INs of the slaves.

So what's the big deal about using multiple MIDI OUTs, other than to impress your friends with big words? Understand that MIDI is a *serial* language. That is a fancy way of saying that MIDI messages get sent down the cable one at a time. A sequencer, to play a single note, has to tell the keyboard "I have a note on. It's note number 55. The key went down this fast." Each of these messages gets sent down the MIDI cable one at a time. But what does this have to do with multiple outs?

Ever been in a traffic jam? Too many cars in too little space and what happens, besides lots of car horns and colorful language? The traffic stops. The same thing can happen in a MIDI cable. Too much information going down the cable at one time can jam just like the freeway. By spreading out the "traffic" of information over more than one MIDI cable, you can avoid the congestion and keep the traffic flowing. If you are using a large number of MIDI instruments, use of a sequencer with multiple MIDI OUT ports can keep the data flowing down the cables.

Whew! What a lot of ground to cover. But don't worry. To hook up a sequencer, just follow the diagrams and you shouldn't get into too much trouble. If you are having trouble, read on, MacDuff.

6

Don't Panic!

MIDI SYSTEMS AREN'T MAGIC. The phase of the moon won't affect them, nor will any incense or incantations. The reason a problem occurs will almost always be something logical that was overlooked. If you're like me, your forehead may get a little damaged from the "Why didn't I notice that before?" syndrome.

BEING OF SOUND MIND

Listed below and on the following page are variations on the most basic problem: failure to produce a sound. The possible causes are given, along with solutions to correct them. For a comprehensive discussion of MIDI troubleshooting, see *What's MIDI?* by Jon F. Eiche (Hal Leonard Publishing, 1990).

If your instruments are making no sound at all:

- Are they connected to an audio amplifier and are all volume knobs turned up? (You, there in the back, quit snickering! This may sound funny, but it's happened to all of us at some point in time.)

31

If one of the slave units is making no sound:

- Are the MIDI connections correct? Is there a bad cable? Double check the connections and connect a cable you know is good.

- Are all components of the system turned on? If a unit isn't on, it can't pass MIDI data through to the THRU port, which will result in inactive instruments in a daisy chain.

- Are the MIDI channel assignments correct? Double check them.

- Check to see if the sequencer's *soft thru* function (also called *echo back*, or *patch thru*) is on. This feature turns the MIDI OUT port into both an OUT and a THRU. It is used to allow you to hear the slaves when recording from the master.

Most of the time, a problem is something simple that has been overlooked. Don't panic, breathe deeply, and dive in calmly. Remember, there's nothing magic about MIDI.

7

Is a pilot's license necessary to operate a box with so many buttons on it?

HARDWARE SEQUENCERS COME IN A VARIETY of shapes, sizes, colors, and prices. Some look like the control panel of a jet fighter, while others have only a few tiny buttons on a deceptively simple looking front panel. They vary greatly in features and how you interact with them.

IN THE CHANNEL, ON THE TRACK

Before we look more closely at features, we need to clarify a couple of terms. When the word *channel* is used, it is implied that a MIDI channel is being discussed. When the word *track* is used, it is a recording/playback track on a sequencer. Why should you know the difference? What is the difference, anyway?

Hardware sequencers usually have from two to eight tracks in which you can place data. For instance, on a four-track sequencer, it is possible to record data on four tracks. Does this

33

mean that on a four-track sequencer you are limited to recording four parts? No!! Manufacturers want you to have more flexibility than that. But how do the extra parts fit into only four tracks?

MIDI data are generally associated with a specific MIDI channel. Data recorded into a sequencer will be played back on a specific MIDI channel. Only instruments set to that specific channel will respond to that data. Manufacturers have designed most hardware units so that it is possible to record MIDI data from multiple MIDI channels onto a single sequencer track. (See why the distinction between track and channel is important now?) Each MIDI channel corresponds to a separate instrumental part.

For example, on that hypothetical four-track sequencer, track 1 might have three different parts recorded on it, on MIDI channels 1, 2, and 5. The other tracks could have additional parts on different (or the same) MIDI channels.

THE BASIC FOOD GROUPS

All external sequencers can be put into two basic groups:

- Models that have have a single record track.

- Models that have multiple record tracks.

In the first kind of sequencer, all recording must happen on a single track specified by the manufacturer. After recording a part on that track, the data must be transferred to another track before another part is recorded. If you don't transfer the data, the old track will be "written over" when you record the next part, and you will lose the original data. So these are actually two-track sequencers, but only one track can be used for recording. The other is used for storage of information after it is recorded. The following illustration spells out the recording procedure:

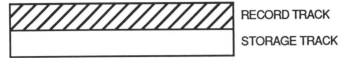

1. The first part is recorded onto the RECORD TRACK.

2. The data from the RECORD TRACK are transferred to the STORAGE TRACK.

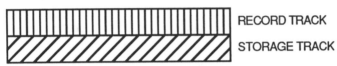

3. The second part is recorded onto the RECORD TRACK.

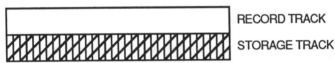

4. The data from the RECORD TRACK are merged with the data on the STORAGE TRACK.

Recording on a two-track sequencer.

Steps 3 and 4 in the illustration are repeated as often as necessary for additional parts. Note that the storage track can contain information from multiple MIDI channels. You haven't lost the flexibility of having multiple MIDI channels. It's just that all the data are placed into a single track.

The other type of sequencer has multiple tracks that can be recorded on. Select the track you want to record on and just do it. To record another part, go to another track and record there. That data can be merged with another track and consolidated onto a single track. It is similar to the two-track design, only more flexible.

Many multitrack sequencers allow you to put multiple MIDI channels on each track, just as you can with the two-track variety. But there are also sequencers that allow only a single MIDI channel on a single track. These units, however, often have up to eight tracks to record on. If eight parts will be sufficient for you, these models may be all you need.

(Most software sequencers—discussed in Chapter 9—allow only one part per track. But they often have many, many tracks available. In addition, many of them allow you to direct each track to more than one MIDI channel on playback. For example, if you've recorded a part on track 1, you might play it back on MIDI channels 4 and 7 to direct it to two different instruments; but both instruments would play the same notes.)

FIRST EDITION

Also, many sequencers allow you to edit (change) the data within a track. By editing the tracks of a sequence, you can correct any mistakes you might have made while recording. Is Fido still at your feet, waiting to show his undying affection? Made one little tiny mistake in an otherwise flawless and truly inspired performance? No problem! You can correct that mistake from the sequencer to make it perfect. The extent of these editing features will vary from one model of sequencer to the next. Some will allow you to edit nearly any element of a track (and there are a lot of them!) while others will only provide minimal editing facilities.

NEW YEAR'S RESOLUTION

Another consideration when evaluating a sequencer is its timing resolution. This is a fancy way of saying, "Into how many parts does the sequencer divide a quarter note?" Being human, we're never perfectly accurate when we record music into a sequencer. That imperfection is one thing that makes the music feel more human and less mechanical. It is possible to hear even very small deviations in rhythm. The more accurately your sequencer can play back your input (the more divisions it makes per quarter note), the more human the sequencer, and hence the music, will sound. A resolution of 96 parts per quarter note (ppqn) is a respectable minimum standard, though some sequencers go as high as 480 ppqn.

BELLS AND WHISTLES

Sequencers also come with a number of bells and whistles that make the recording process more precise. (Not literal bells or whistles. That's just a figure of speech.) These include *quantization, step-time input, punch-in recording, track shifting,* and *looping.*

Quantization is a fancy word for a process that will correct small rhythmic errors in your playing. Quantizing to a certain note value (usually of your choice) will line up notes in the track to the nearest multiple of that note value. For example, if you quantize a track to 16th notes, all notes in that track will line up exactly on the nearest 16th note. This can be a handy feature to have if your playing needs occasional help.

Step-time input is useful when you are trying to record a particularly difficult section. It allows you to enter notes one at a time, while the sequencer waits patiently after each note for you to enter the next one. It is an alternative to real-time recording (normal recording-as-you-play). With step-time recording, you can enter music that is too complex for real-time entry, or that is too difficult for you to play technically.

37

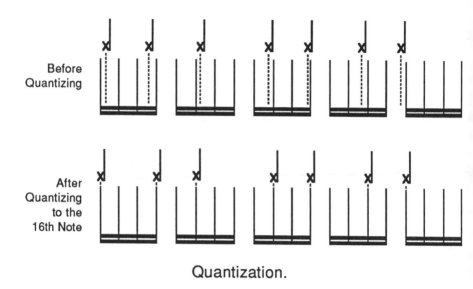

Before
Quantizing

After
Quantizing
to the
16th Note

Quantization.

If this step-time business sounds familiar, it's because it is a throwback to the early sequencers mentioned in Chapter 4. It just goes to show that sometimes the best ideas are old ones.

What happens when you have entered a part but want to rerecord a single measure somewhere in the middle of the song? Enter punch-in recording. This feature will turn the Record button on and off automatically at points you specify. No more reaching over to try and hit the Stop button before you record over parts you want to keep. You can tell the sequencer when to "press" Record and when to turn it off.

Track shifting allows you to move a track forward or backward in time, relative to the other tracks. You can generally move the track by measures, beats, clocks (the parts per quarter note discussed earlier), or any combination of the three. Moving by clocks is often important in establishing the proper "feel" for a track. For example, if you decide that your piano part sounds better as a mellow string part, you may need to shift the track ahead to compensate for the slow attack of the strings, so they don't sound "behind the beat." The greater the timing resolution of the sequencer, the more precise you can be in shifting a track.

Looping is a feature that is used to repeat a specified section. You can specify the beginning and end points of the loop and the number of times you wish the loop to play. If you want to play back a chorus twice, for instance, set the loop and let the sequencer do the work. This can cut down the number of notes you play in when you are recording a track.

PATTERNS 'N' MORE

A feature similar to looping is pattern-based recording. Some sequencers, and almost all drum machines, use this approach. A pattern, usually one to four measures in length, is repeated by the machine. You add new parts on the fly as you build the pattern layer by layer. In a drum machine, for instance, record the bass drum the first time through the pattern. Then add the snare drum as the machine repeats the pattern. Keep adding things until you have finished the pattern. Then go on to record the remaining patterns and link them together to form a song.

A related approach found in some sequencers allows you to record individual *sequences* which can then be assembled into *songs*. For example, a pop ballad might consist of five sequences: an intro, a verse, a chorus, a bridge, and an ending. Each of these would only have to be recorded once. But when assembled into a song, they could be played back in any order, any number of times. For example: intro, verse, verse, chorus, verse, chorus, bridge, chorus, chorus, ending.

SLIPPED DISK

Once you have recorded and polished a sequence, you probably will want to store it somehow. Many sequencers have a *disk drive* built in that lets you save and load sequences quickly and easily. Others have no internal means of storage, but must be connected to either a special external disk storage device (usually using MIDI ports and cables for the connection) or a cassette tape recorder.

These are just a few of the features that may be on a particular model of sequencer. When shopping, don't be afraid to ask questions about the features of a particular unit. Read the manual and advertising to see if a specific sequencer will be right for you.

8

I can hook it all up.
Now what do I do?

SO YOU BOUGHT A SEQUENCER. Now what do you do? This
chapter will give you some practical tips in dealing with a MIDI
sequencing system and tell you about some advanced features
that your sequencer may have.

THANKS FOR THE MEMORY

One of the most important considerations when working with
a sequencer is wise use of the available memory. Although a
sequencer may claim to have the capacity for 10,000 notes, you
may find yourself running out of memory more quickly than
you expect. When you run out of memory, you run out of
room to record more notes. But how can this be? Did you
misjudge the number of notes? Is the unit defective? No, you
just need to take a little closer look at the MIDI language.

For a part to be played via MIDI, remember that there is more
information than just the notes that is recorded. Along with
keeping track of which keys are pressed and how fast, the
sequencer records aftertouch (how much pressure is put on the

key after it is pressed), the pressing and releasing of the sustain pedal, any movement of the mod wheel or pitch bender, and other such information. (This assumes that the instrument is transmitting this information in the first place; not all instruments transmit all of these kinds of MIDI data.) It is all this extra traffic that eats up available memory. When you read that the sequencer can record 10,000 notes, what it really means is 10,000 *events* . If no other data were recorded, the unit could record 10,000 notes. But all this other "stuff" counts as events as well. So where does that leave you? Fear not and tarry awhile longer.

MEMORY CONSERVATION CONVERSATION

Sequencers often give you the option of filtering out or thinning certain types of data. Using this option will decrease the amount of information with which the sequencer must deal with and will free up valuable memory. There is no point in recording data that isn't necessary. Aftertouch, usually used to add vibrato, isn't needed on a pipe organ track. Save that memory and filter that data out. Pitch bend messages can often be thinned (some of them removed) with no audible difference in the sound. Not only does this free up space in memory, it will also cut down on the dreaded clog of MIDI data that may happen in a large sequencing system.

Looping, pattern-based sequencing, and the sequences-linked-as-a-song approach, discussed in Chapter 7, also conserve memory by allowing you to record something once (and consequently store it in memory only once), but have it play back several times as needed.

TREATS FOR FIDO AND AUNT MILLIE

Another useful function on most sequencers is the ability to copy and paste data from one region of a sequence to another. If you are recording a section of music that will repeat 67 times, there is no point in going through the drudgery of playing that section 67 times. Besides, Fido still loves you and editing out all the mistakes will only make you crazy. Copy the repeated section and paste it in the appropriate places. (For all you smart folks out there, you could also loop it in this case, if your sequencer has this ability.) If that special piano part happens again in another part of the song, copy the part and paste it in where needed.

Transposition is another nifty little thing your sequencer may have available. This feature lets you change the key of a song, or parts of a song, in the sequencer. For instance, pop songs often repeat the final chorus in a key higher than in the rest of the song. Use the copy and paste function to copy the chorus and paste it at the end of the sequence. Then use the transpose function to place the final chorus in the new key. Does Aunt Millie want to sing along but can't quite reach the high notes? Transpose the song into a key in which she can sing.

MINDING (AND MENDING) YOUR PATCH CHANGES

The sequencer can also record patch changes for you. Rather than setting each instrument to the desired sound by hand, have the sequencer do it for you. A rather strong word of caution, however. Let those who have ears—Listen Up! If you are using a two-track sequencer of the type discussed in the Chapter 7, be careful about inserting or recording patch changes into the sequence. Once the data have been taken from the record track and placed into the storage track, no changes can be made. Once you have transferred any part containing a patch change to the storage track, you are committed to that patch change. Nothing can be done to extract the data and change your mind. The sound you have chosen will be the sound your keyboard or module will preselect, no matter what. The only alternatives are:

1. Set the sounds by hand quickly after the patch change commands have been sent—an impractical and almost silly procedure.

2. Record these manual patch changes into the record track and then merge them into the storage track. Then when the sequence plays back it will send out two patch changes in quick succession—first the wrong one, then the right one.

3. If the instrument is programmable (a synthesizer, for example), put the right sound in the location that is selected by the recorded patch change.

4. Trash the sequence and start over.

None of these is a very good option. Be careful.

Another aspect of sequenced patch changes that needs careful attention has to do with the processing time of the instrument itself. Depending on the model of instrument you are using, the time it takes to process and execute a patch change can be quite long—up to a second on some instruments. While a second isn't usually considered a long time, it is an eternity while you are waiting for a new sound to come up on your keyboard or module. The instrument can't play any notes during this time. The musical flow of a piece can be thoroughly destroyed by a thoughtless patch change. Plan ahead and allow enough time for the instrument to process the patch change command. Wait for a spot where the particular instrument isn't playing before inserting a patch change command. With a heavy flow of MIDI data, patch changes need to be purposely and thoughtfully planned.

MULTIPLE PERSONALITIES

To give you more for your dollar, many manufacturers are creating instruments that are *multitimbral*. This is a fancy way of saying that the instrument will play more than one sound at a time. These different sounds can be set to different MIDI channels, an ideal situation for sequencing. You don't need a separate keyboard or module for each sound you want. By setting up these wonder boxes, you can get sounds such as strings, piano, bass, and even drums out of one instrument. Simply set each part to the appropriate sound you want and go.

Unfortunately, every silver cloud has a dark lining. (Well, maybe not every one.) One of the most important things to keep track of when using a multitimbral unit (or any MIDI instrument, for that matter) is the number of notes available. An instrument cannot produce more notes than it was designed to. If the keyboard was built to play 16 notes and the piano part needs 14 of those notes in a particular spot, only 2 notes will be left for whatever other parts may be playing there. The polyphony (number of notes) is divided among the different parts. It's annoying to listen to an otherwise wonderful sequence, only to find notes missing in it because it is trying to play too many notes at the same time.

CHASING RAINBOWS

One of the most baffling phenomena in the wonderful world of MIDI has a number of symptoms. What in the world could cause these horrific results:

1. You stop somewhere in the middle of a sequence, fast-forward several measures, and upon starting again your keyboard is suddenly out of tune.

2. You start somewhere in the middle of the sequence only to find that your well planned and up to now flawless patch changes are seemingly worthless because the parts are being played by the wrong sounds.

The cause of both these symptoms is quite simple and with some sequencers quite easy to correct.

Suppose you have recorded a sequence and have placed patch change commands at the beginning. These patch changes are flawless, until you start in the middle of the sequence. By starting in the middle of the sequence, after the patch changes, these commands are never sent to the instrument. The instrument can't change patches if the sequencer doesn't tell it to do so. That is, without a feature called *event chasing*.

Event chasing is a handy little option that will scan data in the sequence prior to the start point. Scanning automatically for certain MIDI commands, it will tell the sequencer to send commands to the instruments prior to starting playback. For instance, with event chasing on and set to scan for patch changes, the sequencer will look at the sequence, find the closest prior patch change command in each part and send it automatically. This feature can scan for patch changes, pitch bend commands (the cause of the keyboard being out of tune), and many other MIDI commands and controllers. It can save a lot of head scratching and hours of frustration spent trying to solve a problem with a simple cause.

A DIFFERENT DRUMMER

Another possible source of confusion can result from the use of a drum machine. (Not that the use of the drum machine itself will make you inherently confused.) Some quite interesting, though most often not musical, things can result from drum machines that are not synchronized correctly to the sequencer. Here is our scenario: You have programmed your drum machine to play the drum part for your latest sequence. Trying to play everything back doesn't quite work, though. The drums are playing one tempo and the sequencer another one. What is the matter?

The sequencer, when the Play button is pushed, sends out a command that says in plain English, "Start." That triggers the

Play button for units such as drum machines. Where trouble can creep in, though, is in the synchronization of the drum machine to the sequencer. If the drum machine isn't being told by the sequencer how fast to go, it will go on its merry way, playing at its own tempo. The drum machine's "clock" needs to be set to receive the timing information from the sequencer. Its clock needs to be set to "MIDI," or "External." With the drum machine in this mode, it will receive the commands from the sequencer to keep it playing at the same tempo.

GET TO THE POINT(ER)

In addition to synchronization, there is another potential snare in using a drum machine. If you want to start a sequence somewhere in the middle, how will the drum machine know where to start? It gets the "Start" command from the sequencer all right, but remember, you aren't starting at the beginning. The drum machine needs to be told where the sequencer is starting in order for it to start in the right place as well. The MIDI Song Position Pointer command does just that. This is a command that is sent out saying, "I'm at measure 27." A Song Position Pointer message will tell the drum machine to start at the correct spot, while the MIDI clock (synchronization) commands will keep the drum machine and sequencer in perfect time.

DRIVING DRUMS

You say your drum machine doesn't respond to Song Position Pointer commands? You may have to start from the beginning of the sequence in order for the drum machine to begin at the correct place. Then again, you may have some options. It will take a small shift in your thinking, but there is an alternative. Instead of synchronizing the drum machine and sequencer, use the sequencer to play the drum machine. In other words, use the drum machine as a source of drums sounds, just as you would use a keyboard for other sounds. (For this to work, the drum machine must be able to respond to incoming MIDI note data. Most do.)

This approach completely solves the Song Position Pointer problem. It isn't much more work, and allows you to edit the drum track from the sequencer itself. The down side is the need to deal with a little more information on your part and the potential MIDI jam that more data may cause.

There are two approaches to using your sequencer to drive the drum machine as a sound module:

- You can program the machine as you normally would and then record the drum track into the sequencer, making sure the two units are properly synchronized.

- You can create a drum track right from the sequencer, triggering the drums from your keyboard. (The note assignments will vary drastically from one machine to another. If playing middle C triggers the snare sound on one machine, it will most likely not trigger the snare on a different machine.)

Recording drums "live" is best done in several passes. Playing an entire drum set live from a keyboard is a monumental feat. It is much easier to record basic drums first (kick and snare, for example), followed by cymbals and other parts on one or more other tracks, and finally merging everything together.

The subject of sequencing is a vast one. Only the proverbial surface has been scratched here. Each sequencer has unique features and approaches. But with the basic knowledge you now have, you can ask intelligent questions and read the manuals with more understanding. Now that you have this wonderful wisdom, let's talk about the high-powered world of computer–based sequencers.

9

Computer-based sequencing: Your computer is more than a fancy electronic typewriter

IF YOU ALREADY OWN A PERSONAL COMPUTER, a software sequencer may be the best route to take for your sequencing needs. It may save you money and provide you with a more powerful system, albeit a less portable one, than a hardware device. Sequencing software is available for all common personal computers, ranging in features from the very simple to the very powerful.

DISK-GO HERE, DISK-GO THERE

When you buy a software sequencer, you are buying a disk that contains a computer program. This program contains instructions that tell the machine how to handle instructions you give it, such as strokes from the keyboard or clicks from a mouse. It also contains commands that tell the computer how to draw the screen you are looking at and where to store the information you give it. It contains the information it needs to perform all of its various functions.

This is similar to the hardware sequencers discussed previously. They also contain a program that tells them how to operate. The difference between the two, however, is significant. With a hardware sequencer, the instructions are stored permanently in the machine's circuitry. To put in a new set of instructions, or program, the integrated circuit chips that store the program must be exchanged for new chips containing the new program. This is something usually left to qualified service personnel at a service center for your brand of sequencer. With a computer-based unit, updating the program is as easy as plugging in a new disk. (A few hardware sequencers also load their software from a disk.) New versions of software usually add new features to the program, as well as fix problems, called *bugs*, from the previous version.

ABOUT (INTER)FACE

In addition to the software, you will need a MIDI interface that is compatible with your brand of computer. (A MIDI interface is not necessary for those computers that have MIDI ports built in.) A MIDI interface provides the computer with MIDI ports and takes care of the transfer of data between the MIDI devices and the computer. In other words, it makes sure that information from the instruments doesn't collide with information from the computer. Interfaces also come in a variety of configurations. They can be as simple as a one-input/one-output device or can be a full-blown eight-in/eight-out with data filtering, channelizing, event muting, and generation of several species of time code for synchronization to an audio or video tape deck. Your uses of your equipment should determine which features, and hence which interface, you need. You shouldn't buy more power than you need, although you never can tell when a certain feature will save you time and a few headaches. Be realistic in the evaluation of your needs, so that six weeks down the line you aren't saying, "I really wish I had a Widget so I could..."

WITH A VIEW TOWARD FLEXIBILITY

One of the advantages of using a software sequencer is the flexibility (usually) in editing MIDI data. The ability to see large amounts of data in a variety of forms can make the sequencer easier to use than a hardware model. No more squinting at tiny LCD (liquid crystal display) screens and going through page after page of readouts to find a certain parameter. On a computer, you can find most of what you need right there on the screen or access it with a single keystroke or mouse click. It can be a great time saver to access and view information in large doses. It can also be important to see how a certain piece of data is related to another. Seeing this all on one screen can give you a better perspective on your entire sequence.

Software sequencers usually allow a user to view MIDI data in a few different forms as well. For instance, the notes of a track can be edited using an *event list*. In an event list, all MIDI events, such as note information, pitch bend, and any MIDI controller data, are listed in the order they are performed. Here is a portion of an event list:

Event list.

51

Another way to view MIDI data is in *graphic notation*. In this form, notes are displayed as bars on a grid. The length of a note is shown by the length of the bar. The longer the bar, the longer the note. Other information, such as pitch bend and note velocity, is displayed either on the grid with the note information or below it in a separate area of the screen. Here is the same set of notes as seen in graphic notation:

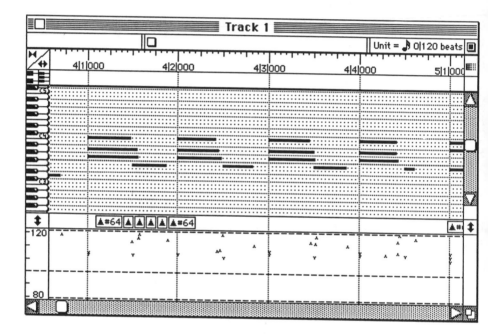

Graphic notation.

A recent feature that can make some editing even easier is *notation* editing. Here, MIDI note messages are displayed as notes on a normal musical staff. Other MIDI information is usually displayed below the staff, much like the graphic editing mode.

Here the same notes again, displayed in notation editing:

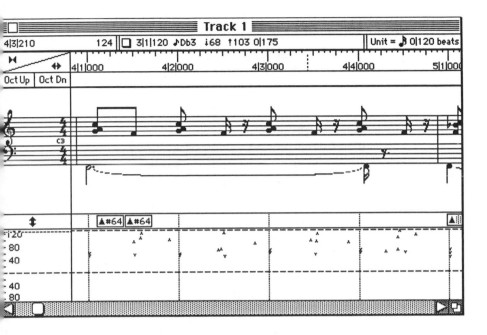

Music notation.

SO WHAT?

All right, so why go through all the trouble of seeing the same thing in three different forms? What's all the commotion about? Well, not only can you view the data in the form of your choice, but you can also view it in the form that will make it the easiest to edit. Each of these views makes certain tasks easier to perform. Different modes have their merits as well as their drawbacks.

Event lists are sequential. The events that are listed are displayed in the order they are performed. (MIDI is serial in nature. MIDI commands are sent one at a time, but fast enough that events can sound like they happen at the same time.) This can be handy for things such as pedaling commands. For instance, suppose you want to make sure the last chord in a measure is held with the sustain pedal. An event list will tell you exactly where the pedal command is in relation to the chord. If the pedal command is listed before the note commands for the chord, the pedal command is sent before the note commands are sent. Hence, the notes of the chord will be held by the pedal. By viewing things in the order they occur, you can make sure that events happen in the order you want them to.

Graphic editing makes viewing the lengths of notes easy, as well as viewing controller events such as pitch bend. For instance, if a single note in a chord is playing longer than it should, graphic editing will let you solve the problem easily. By viewing the notes graphically, you can easily see which note is longer (literally longer on the screen) and adjust its length accordingly. Graphic editing can also make changing the shape of a pitch bend as simple as redrawing the shape of the bend on the screen. Does the bend go too far down? Redraw its shape to decrease the depth right there on the screen.

Notation editing is a recent addition to sequencers. It is usually similar in look to the graphic editing screen. But instead of notes presented on a graph, they are shown as notes on a musical staff. Finding wrong notes is a simple process if you can see them as real notes on a real staff. Looking for the note that just doesn't sound right? Look at the screen and find the note that doesn't fit. Editing other things, such as pitch bend or modulation controls, will usually look the same as in the graphic editing mode.

Features, Bugs, and Algorithms

The flexibility of a software sequencer also pays in the "guess what new feature they will add this week" game. New features and the occasional software bug can be all taken care of with a new disk containing the update.

There is an offshoot of the standard software sequencer known as *algorithmic composition software*. These programs will "compose" music according to parameters you set up in the program. For example, you tell the program what notes to use (what keys or scale), what rhythmic values to use, and the tempo, and let the computer go to work. Other such programs take musical material that you provide and modify it within limits that you specify. While traditional musicians may scoff at this approach to music making, the programs are quite detailed and allow the user a great deal of control over the result. By making careful and thoughtful choices, you can bring some beautiful and very creative music to life using these composition tools.

WEIGHING THE EVIDENCE

There are both advantages and disadvantages to software sequencers as compared to hardware units. Your particular needs will determine which is appropriate for you. Hardware units, which do not need to do the internal "housekeeping" chores that computers must (displaying the screen, scanning the keyboard, etc.), can load sequences more quickly. If you will be using the sequencer in live performance, this may a consideration. There is nothing quite so uncomfortable as waiting for your sequencer to boot up on stage. A personal computer and sequencing software, however, have the advantage in ease and flexibility of data editing. A hardware unit won't do word processing, spreadsheets, or video games, either.

Performers should be aware that computers usually require more time to set up and pack up than hardware sequencers. They also take up more space and generally are less roadworthy. Musicians who have the money sometimes use a computer to create and edit sequences at home or in the studio, then record them into a hardware unit for use on the road.

Out-troduction

SEQUENCING TRULY IS A BIG TOPIC. Only the surface has been scratched here. A sequencer is a musical instrument, and as such it takes practice and patience to master. With the basic knowledge you've gained here, you know enough to ask the right questions. No sequencer is the same as another. All the different brands and models have different features and advantages. The choice will be up to you.

Take the time to learn about and master your sequencer. It can be a valuable tool in your music making. It is a tool that can make your music more exciting and alive. But, just like many other things, you will only get out of it what you put into it. A sequencer can help you create music more quickly and easily. But just because it's faster and easier doesn't mean it's good. A sequencer won't make the music good or bad. That part is still up to you.

There isn't any magic to it, just a little time and patience. But the results of some good hard work can be very satisfying. Enjoy!

About the Author

GREG STARR has served as an arranger, writer, and editor for Hal Leonard Publishing since 1989. Hailing from the Pacific Northwest, he previously taught math and electronic music courses at a junior college. He has also been known to moonlight as a lounge lizard.

In addition to working with pen (or computer) and paper, he applies his knowledge of sequencing and synthesis to produce recordings for Hal Leonard.

Greg is married, but he does not own a dog named Fido or have an aunt named Millie.

Index

YOUR ANSWERS TO UNDERSTANDING THE NEW MUSIC TECHNOLOGY